MW00529410

RAGS
to
RENTAL PROPERTY

KIRK T. McGARY

Fulton Books, Inc.
Meadville, PA

Published by Fulton Books 2021

ISBN 978-1-63860-106-7 (paperback)
ISBN 978-1-63860-297-2 (hardcover)
ISBN 978-1-63860-107-4 (digital)

Printed in the United States of America

To my wife Blenda, children, and
grandchildren, who make life worth living.

CONTENTS

CHAPTER 1

Quality of Life

Bill used to stop by my office every month to pay his rent on the home he was renting from us. He would give his rent to the receptionist then make his way into my office to say hi. He would then proceed to give me his monthly speech: "When I retire, I'm going to sell everything I have, buy a motor home, and travel all over the country, seeing the sights with my wife. It'll be great!"

That day finally came, and Bill, still renting from us after all those years, stopped into my office to tell me he had officially retired and he had purchased a new motor home. He proceeded to tell me that he and his wife were leaving the next week for a mini "test trip" to Yellowstone Park in the new motor home.

The following month, Bill's wife stopped in the office to pay rent. I saw her and asked her how the Yellowstone trip went and how Bill was doing. The tears flowed. She related that a couple of days after they returned from Yellowstone, Bill had a heart attack and passed away.

I felt their pain. They had worked and saved for decades to fulfill their dreams, and now it was over—albeit with unfulfilled dreams.

Do not drive down Bill's road! Get your act together now. Do not wait "until the market improves" or say, "I need to save up more money for a down payment," or any other lame excuse. You can do it, like me and thousands of other real estate investors.

Money solves many problems and creates many opportunities. If you work fifteen hours a day, seven days a week, you can probably earn quite a bit of money. But you will have limited time to use it, and ultimately, your health will start to fail if you continue living at that frantic pace for an extended period. In other words, there are three aspects to having a great quality of life: health, time, and money.

Health. Several years ago, we were having an extended family reunion in our backyard. The younger kids were screaming in the swimming pool and playing games, the seniors were huddled under the pavilion swapping stories of the good ole days, and the rest of us thirty-to-sixty-year-olds were sliding down a 150-foot-long waterslide we had set up on the side of the hill, which ended in a giant pool of water in the apple orchard.

With the smell of hamburgers and hot dogs in the air, this was the perfect day—food, fun, and family.

And then the unthinkable happened.

As I was walking by the pavilion toward the swimming pool, I had this pain and pulsating feeling going down my left arm, from my heart to the tip of my middle finger. Could this be real? Was I actually having a heart attack? But I was only in my fifties then!

After a day in the hospital and an angiogram, echocardiogram, and numerous other tests; I, it was determined, had not had a heart attack. Instead, the fast-paced lifestyle of the previous twenty years of my being a CEO was catching up with me.

As I started to modify my work schedule, travel schedule, etc., I fully realized that without health to enjoy life, simply having lots of money was not going to provide a great quality of life; health is critical.

Time. A colleague of mine has been a doctor for many years. As a surgeon, he earns quite a lot of money. One day, he asked me how I could take so much time off work to travel and participate in so many non-work-related activities like boating, gardening, traveling, doing service, attending college games, etc. He then proceeded to tell me that he was on call every other weekend, and if he was not in the operating room, he was not earning any money.

What good is lots of money if you cannot spend it doing the things you want to do because there is no time? Is all your time tied to your job? Is all your income tied to your job? Is all your life completely tied to your job? If so, it's time you take control of your time.

Money. If you had lots of money, how would you use it? Would you buy lots of toys, save it all for a rainy day, pay off your mortgage, or buy tickets to the Lakers game? The options are limitless, so it is important to determine your goals, needs, and wants. Once you have a money road map, then it becomes easier to plan and take action.

Real estate investing is an amazing vehicle for you to accomplish your goals. Did you know that as of 2019, about 90 percent of millionaires had become millionaires by investing in real estate, and 10 percent of billionaires?

You can do it! Yes, even average, you can do it. Let's take the journey.

CHAPTER 2

Benefits of Investing in Real Estate

So here we go—ten great reasons to invest in real estate.

Passive Income vs. Active Income

Perhaps one of the best things about earning income from rental property is that you earn money whether you go to work or not. At the first of each month, the rent money comes in, and then you can use it to pay the mortgage, save for another down payment for your next rental property, or perhaps start to pay off some old nagging bills. And there is no cap on how many rentals you can buy. The more you purchase, the more you make, especially in the long-term.

Monthly Cash Flow

Most rental properties these days will rent for more than the cost of the monthly mortgage if you finance the property. Thus, the excess monies you collect can be used for various things. First, I would save at least two months' worth of rent for a rainy day. Rainy-day items can include the tenant being late on rent or the need to replace the water heater. After you have saved two months' worth of rent (which you can probably do within six to twelve months), then the monies can be used for other purposes. Do not waste this money; use it to pay off old debts or save for a down payment on your next rental property.

Tax Advantages

1. As noted earlier, most millionaires got to be millionaires by owning real estate. Over the past ten years, if you have purchased almost any real estate, its value will have increased significantly since you bought it. Let us assume you purchased a small property for $250,000, rented it out for the past three years, and now it is worth $350,000. If you sell the property, the gain— $350,000 less the cost of $250,000—would yield you approximately $100,000 of profit. But unlike your paycheck, which is taxed at higher ordinary income rates, this $100,000 gain that is going into your pocket is taxed at capital gain rates—significantly lower than ordinary income rates. Currently, the highest capital gain rate is 20 percent, while the highest ordinary income rate is 37.6 percent. That's $17,600 less you will have to pay in taxes!

A second tax advantage is converting some items to business expense. Typically, you would create an LLC company to take title to the property. This is a fairly easy process, costing only a couple of hundred dollars and providing you with some liability protection as well. Let's say the property needs new blinds and a couple of garden hoses. You can take the used ones from your existing home, convert them to business use at their fair market value, and now deduct the value from your taxes. The tax money that you will save can help purchase the new blinds or hoses going back to your home. There are numerous items you can do this with.

Also, if you go to work on the property or drive by to inspect, your travel costs now become tax-deductible.

Note that the rental income is taxed not at capital gain rates but at ordinary income tax rates. However, all expenses and depreciation are netted against the income to help reduce the amount of tax you will pay. Depreciation typically is calculated by taking the cost of the property, less the cost of the ground or lot, and dividing it currently by 27.5 years (dictated by the IRS Code). In the example we used above, let's assume of the $250,000 paid for the property, the cost of the ground was $50,000. Thus, we would take $250,000 less the cost of the lot of $50,000, which equals $200,000. We then take the $200,000, divide it by 27.5 years, and that gives us a $7,272 tax write-off per year for the next twenty-seven years! If the overall property shows a loss, it will generally offset your income from your job, saving you lots of tax dollars.

Anything that you purchase directly for the property is, of course, tax-deductible as well.

Appreciation

Since cavemen and cave women have owned caves, real estate has continued to increase in value. Sure, there have been times when real estate has decreased in value, but if you have purchased correctly, you can ride out the slowdowns and take advantage of the appreciation in value over the years.

Let's look at a simple example. Assume that you purchased a $300,000 property and that its value increases just 5 percent per year. After five years, the value of the property is $382,884; you have gained over $82,000 in value, not including the rental income, for the past five years! If the property were held for ten years with 5 percent appreciation each year, the value is a whopping $488,668—over $188,000!

Leverage

Leverage, in this sense, is when you use debt or a mortgage to purchase a property. In the example above, let's assume you put 10 percent down and borrowed the rest for the purchase of the $300,000 property. This would mean you put $30,000 down and borrowed $270,000.

If we just look at the return on your investment of the $30,000 down payment in relation to the appreciation, you have made $82,884 ÷ $30,000 = 276 percent ÷ 5 years = 55-percent-per-year return on your money invested. That's impressive! And we have not even considered the rental income or the fact that the tenant's money is paying down the mortgage each month, thus increasing your equity in the property even more.

What if you purchased two or three or eleven of these properties? The numbers get very interesting. But borrowing certainly comes with some risk. That is why you must purchase the properties correctly, which we will cover later in this book. As long as you purchase correctly, you can weather mostly any downturn in the economy.

Hedge against Inflation and Recession

As inflation heats up and items become more costly, so does real estate. If you own real estate, the value of your asset generally increases more than the rate of inflation. Thus, your value is protected and usually enhanced during inflationary times.

In a recession, quite often, rents will decrease a little bit. But if you have a tenant on a lease, the rent will not change until the end of the lease. Even then, the tenant may choose to renew at the previous rate versus go through the effort of moving.

Or even looking at a worst-case scenario, you may have to lower your rent a little bit. It should be noted that during recessionary times, the number of tenants needing a place to live increases, partially due to the fact the prospective tenants (former homeowners) can no longer afford to own or purchase a house. Thus, they have become a tenant, increasing the demand for rental properties and thus helping to maintain higher rents.

Value Never Goes Away

With some non-real estate investments, oftentimes the value of your investment can actually go to zero. For example, if you purchase a stock and the company goes under, the value of your stock can actually be zero. With real estate, the value can decrease for various reasons, but it doesn't go to zero. If you need to sell it for some reason, there will almost always be someone that will pay a reduced price for the property.

More Difficult to Be Defrauded

Real estate is a tangible asset. In other words, you can see it, touch it, move into it, rent it, sell it, and keep it. Though there have been many scams and bad deals, it is more difficult to hide or conceal things with real estate. Later in this book, we will discuss assembling your trusted team of experts that will help you avoid some of the potential pitfalls.

Tenants Pay the Mortgage for You

Wouldn't it be great if someone else paid off your property for you? They will! Each month, the tenants of the property pay you their rent. You, in turn, use their money to then submit your mortgage payment. Over the course of the years, your mortgage will be paid off by using the tenants' rent money each month; it doesn't come from your pocket.

Real Estate versus Other Types of Investment

There are a host of investments that you can put your money into, like gold, silver, bonds, antiques, CDs (certificate of deposits), stocks, and real estate. Many individuals have made millions in each of these investment vehicles. Equally, many people have lost millions in each of these investment vehicles as well. So it isn't simply that one is better than another; it is more about which vehicle fits your purposes better.

Typically, precious metals, such as gold and silver, work well and retain their value in difficult economic times. During the COVID-19 pandemic, both metals increased significantly in value. But neither generates monthly cash flow that you can spend, nor are there any assurances that they will be worth more money a year later. The only time you can get money out of them is when you sell them or trade them for something else of value.

Bonds are financial vehicles typically issued by government entities like counties, cities, school districts, etc. They are also issued by companies. Bonds, quite often, will pay some amount of interest during the life of the bond, then the principal is paid back at the end of the term of the bond. Their face value will fluctuate based on the economy and interest rates. If interest rates increase, the value of the bond decreases because other bonds become available at a higher-earning interest rate. If interest rates decrease, the value of the bond typically will increase because the bond has a higher fixed rate of income than new bonds; therefore, people are willing to pay more for the bond. The yields on bonds vary but can run from less than 1 percent to 10 percent. In general, bonds are a more conservative investment, thus returning modest gains on your investment.

Antiques are very unique. If you are an expert in paintings, art, coins, etc., then you might consider this investment vehicle. Of course, if you are an expert in antiques, then you already understand the risks and returns. Unless you are an expert, I would avoid this risk of your hard-earned money.

CDs, or certificate of deposits, are quite secure and can be purchased at most any bank or credit union. But because of their security, their returns are relatively low. Over the past ten years or so, they have yielded between less than 1 percent and around 4 percent.

Stocks—where do we begin? There are mountains of data and information available and almost an equally large number of stocks and funds to choose from. There are high-risk and high-return stocks, medium-risk and medium-return stocks, and low-risk and low-return stocks. If you venture down this path, make sure you select the very best adviser available. One test might be to see how much the adviser is worth. If they can "help you make millions," then surely, they have made millions themselves. What do you actually control with this investment? Only when you buy and when you sell. You must rely on others—like CEOs, the markets, and the economies of the world—to realize significant gains on your stock investments.

With real estate, you have many options to enhance its value. You control when you buy, when you sell, if you want to upgrade the property, if you want to move into the property, if you want to rent the property, if you want to increase or decrease the rent, if you borrow against the property, if you pay off the property, and a host of other options. You have greater control over its value than you do with most other investment vehicles. You are in the driver's seat versus just along for the ride with other investment vehicles.

═══ CHAPTER 3 ═══

What Are the Types of Real Estate?

So what is your favorite type of potato dish? Having grown up on a potato farm in Idaho, I quickly learned there is a host of different types of potato dishes: baked, au gratin, hash browns, cheesy, funeral (a classic that is worth trying before you depart), raw, soup, chips, bread, salad, twice-baked, mashed, tater tots, and of course, my favorite—french fries.

Like potato dishes, there are various types of real estate that can be purchased: single-family houses, condos, duplexes, fourplexes, multifamily buildings (apartments), office buildings, warehouse buildings, retail buildings, storage units, boat marinas, building lots, nightly vacation rentals, and many more. Each has its own unique rewards and challenges.

So what is right for you or the best way to get started? First, let's break this down into two major categories—residential and commercial (everything else). Residential would consist of any real estate that is used to live in or stay in. This would include single-family, condos, all plexes, apartments, and nightly rentals. Commercial would consist of office space, mall space, warehouses, etc. Let's take a deeper look and see what works for you to consider investing in.

Residential Properties

Single-family. This type of property is a single home. The advantages include that it is the simplest to purchase and typically the easiest to sell when that time comes. It also is one of the easier properties to rent. Families generally prefer to live in a single-family house versus some type of apartment, if they can afford it. Thus, there is a pretty strong demand for this type of rental.

One of the disadvantages is that the return on your investment may not be as high as what you could earn from, let's say, a fourplex. For example, if you purchased a fourplex for $600,000, each of the four rental units cost you $150,000. Let's assume each unit rented for $1,200. Thus, your income would be $4,800 per month or $57,600 per year on a $600,000 investment, which equals 9.6 percent return.

If you purchase a single-family house for $350,000 and it rents for $2,500 per month, the return would be $30,000 of annual rent divided by the $350,000 purchase price, which equals 8.6 percent—slightly less than the fourplex.

Condos. This would be a unit in a condominium complex. It generally will be connected to a number of other units. One of the major advantages to purchasing a condo is that the purchase price is usually lower than a single-family house. However, one of the disadvantages is that you surrender some of your autonomy and you are along for the ride with the condo association. Sometimes, the association may impose rental restrictions or increase condo association fees and the like, and you may have no control over their actions.

Plexes. Let's define what a *plex* is. A *plex* would start with a duplex (two units) and go all the way up to around a fifty-unit building. That would include a fourplex, sevenplex, seventeenplex, thirty-sevenplex, etc., up to a fiftyplex.

For the most part, a plex functions very much like a single-family property—only there are a couple of them hooked together. This is different from a condo in a sense that with a condo, you only own part of the building, i.e., a single unit in the building. In a plex, you own the entire plex, i.e., in a fourplex, you own all four units.

Some of the advantages include controlling the entire building, thus allowing you the ability to buy, sell, rent, or move into the property. Most lenders will be willing to loan monies on real estate up to a fourplex without too many new requirements. Larger plexes will typically require a little more sophistication to get them financed.

In general, the return will be a little bit higher on a plex versus a single-family home. However, due to this same reason, plexes, at bargain prices, are challenging to find. Thus, in many markets, they are nearly impossible to purchase.

Multifamily. These are buildings that contain numerous units, usually fifty or more per building. There are many buildings that will have hundreds of units per building. When I lived in Japan many years ago (Konnichiwa!), I would visit some of the larger complexes. It was like an entire city in a single building! There were literally thousands of people living inside. And often on the first floor, there would be grocery stores, clothing stores, and other retail shops.

So here is the point: the cost of these buildings will be in the tens of millions of dollars or more. Unless you have that kind of money or access to that kind of money, this type of property is probably not for you. Quite often, the players in this market are billion-dollar players. And their level of real estate investing is quite sophisticated. If you are just starting out, this is probably an area to avoid.

Nightly/vacation rentals. Nightly rentals are becoming more and more popular. Even prior to the COVID-19 pandemic, nightly rentals were gaining in popularity. This is evidenced by numerous websites/companies facilitating the renting and ownership of nightly rentals. And since international travel has been reduced due to the pandemic, this type of rental unit has become even more popular.

I was recently staying just outside of West Yellowstone, Montana. Being the real estate junkie that I am, I looked up a number of rental properties to see: first, if they were being fully rented through the summer season, and second, how much the nightly rents were. I was shocked by both answers. There were very few vacancies, and the nightly rates were extremely high. Owners of those rental units are doing quite well.

A couple of years ago, my wife and I purchased a nightly rental just outside the national parks area in southern Utah. We had to do a little upgrading to the property even though it was just four years old. We added furniture, painted the property, and built a swimming pool in the backyard. I'm pleased to report that over the past four months, we haven't had a single vacant night! The nightly rental fees are about four times more money than if we were renting it monthly.

Note that not any house can be used as a nightly rental. Many homeowners' and condo owners' associations don't allow nightly rentals. Also, many cities require a business license to operate a nightly rental. And some cities have stopped issuing permits that would allow you to rent nightly. Don't rely on what a sales agent may tell you about rental licensing; you must verify the ability to rent nightly yourself, with both the HOA/COA and the city/county where the property is located.

Personal residence. A personal residence is usually a sound investment. However, this is the one time that emotional factors come into play, not just number crunching to evaluate the investment. Emotional factors include good neighborhood to raise the kids, safety, close to work, close to family or friends, good access to shopping and recreation, etc.

Many of the same numerical factors apply to purchasing a personal residence, but we also should include the emotional factors when making this decision. It isn't all about the money, though the money is a significant factor.

One of the great advantages to buying a personal residence is the tax advantage. The interest on the mortgage and the property taxes are deductible. But also, the gain on the property's appreciation may be completely nontaxable. Currently, a person can exclude $250,000 of gain from taxes or $500,000 if married—half a million dollars tax-free! This can be done if you have lived in the home two of the previous five years. And this process can be repeated every two years. Also, be sure and keep all receipts for any type of additions you make to your property. These items can be added to the cost of your home and then subtracted from the sales price when you sell it. On paper, this will reduce the amount of your gain, thus reducing any taxes you may have to pay.

Commercial Properties

Commercial properties include office buildings, warehouses, retail buildings, storage units, boat marinas, and many more. Commercial properties have a number of different factors than residential. Quite often, the maintenance costs can be much less as you don't have people spending all night at the property. Thus, kitchens and bathrooms may have much less use than a residence.

However, finding a tenant can be far more difficult. If the property is a three-thousand-square-foot office space, how many prospective tenants are there in that particular market that are looking for that exact type of space? By contrast, if you have a three-thousand-square-foot home, how many prospective tenants are there in that particular market looking for that type of space? No doubt there are many more times residential tenants than commercial tenants.

Commercial property management and leasing are quite different as well. A typical residential lease is for one year, whereas a commercial lease quite often is a five-year lease. And unless you are in the commercial leasing business, you will probably need to hire a commercial leasing agent. They will typically charge around 7 percent of the entire lease amount. For example, if the agent leased the unit at $3,000 per month for sixty months, the rents would equal $180,000; and the 7 percent leasing fee would be $12,600, usually paid at the front end of the lease.

Frequently, the floor plan of the commercial space is not ideal for the new tenant. Thus, the property owner will need to build out an agreed-upon modified floor plan. This can be very costly and take lots of time. The cost must be considered prior to signing the lease. Quite often, the cost of the build-out can be transferred to the new tenant.

Buying vacant land is another form of investing in real estate. When buying an actual building lot, you would want to know how it is zoned with the local county/city. If you want to build a duplex, you must ensure that it is zoned for a duplex.

Once zoning is verified, then you would get bids from several contractors to get an idea of what the cost of your project is going to be. You must then weigh the cost of the lot plus construction cost versus the rent you will be getting from the property. At different times, based on the economy, it can be more effective to build, and sometimes not. You simply need to run all the numbers to see which is best.

Another possible option with building lots is, you purchase them, hold them for a period, and then try to sell them for more. Obviously, this only works well when real estate is moving up at a strong clip. But it should be noted that you have no income on lots and you will pay property tax and insurance. Thus, you will need to be able to absorb the negative cash flow.

You can also buy ground hoping to subdivide it later at a significant profit. This is not for the faint of heart. You must generally go through the difficult process to get the property rezoned. This can literally take years, and in the end, the request for zoning can get denied. One option is to purchase the ground subject to the ability to change the zoning. This type of investment is probably better suited for a more seasoned real estate investor.

A couple of years ago, I purchased a duplex on a very big lot. So I went to the city and "conceptually" asked them if I could divide the lot in half and build another duplex, given that there is ample space and the master zoning plan would accommodate such.

They verbally said the zoning would allow that in that area, so I proceeded with the required paperwork/process to create a small two-lot subdivision. As of this writing, I am still in that process. It has been about one year, and I will be into this process some $10,000. This lot will be worth about $50,000, so the effort is worth it. Nevertheless, it is long, is difficult, and has some risk.

If this is your first foray into real estate investing, I would probably focus on residential investing versus commercial investing or ground purchases. It is somewhat easier to buy residential, easier to rent residential, and easier to sell residential.

Here is a high-level summary of some of the advantages and disadvantages of the various types of real estate investments.

Chart of Investment Types		
Types	Primary Advantages	Primary Disadvantages
Single-family	Easy to buy and sell	Returns may not be as high
Condos	Lower prices	COA fees, regulations
Plexes	Better returns	Higher purchase price
Multifamily	Strong returns	Difficult to purchase, very expensive

Nightly rental	Greater returns	Difficult to find
Personal residence	Fun	Tied to location
Office space	Good returns	Harder to rent
Warehouse space	Good returns	Harder to rent
Retail space	Good returns	Compete against new projects
Storage units	Good returns	Run in cycles for tenants
Building lots	Good returns	Usually a longer-term pay
Ground	Good returns	Has more risk

As you select and build your portfolio of real estate, remember the concept of diversification. For example, if you purchase five different properties in a small mining town and the mine closes, you could be in a little trouble trying to both rent or sell any of your investments.

You should consider diversifying in both the types of property as well as the location. A few years ago, my business partner and I purchased a few office buildings and eighteen residential units. Currently, due to the COVID-19 pandemic, the demand for office space has decreased, given that many people are now working from home. However, the demand for the residential units has skyrocketed during this same period. Thus, we have sold the eighteen units and will reinvest in more residential units in a different state. We will sit on the office buildings until that particular market comes back stronger.

≡ CHAPTER 4 ≡

Finding the Right
Property to Buy

So what is it that we are looking for in our investment property? Well, primarily, it needs to make us a lot of money, right? So we need to consider a number of factors in selecting our purchase. Here are factors to consider.

Location

What is the most common phrase in the real estate industry? Location, location, location! There is an ideal spot for a restaurant in a particular nearby city where I live. It is right off the freeway interchange, across the street from a giant Walmart and numerous other shopping options. So with all this traffic, this spot seems ideal. However, there is only one entrance to the property, and you have to be traveling only northbound to turn into the entrance. And the entrance actually takes you to a strip mall that you have to drive past to get to the actual property. Thus, the southbound, westbound, and eastbound traffic has to drive past the property, turn around, get onto the northbound lanes at a point south of the property, and drive north to the entrance to the strip mall to get something to eat. Since the first burger-and-fries diner opened and died at that location, a Mexican restaurant has come and gone, an Italian restaurant has come and gone (too bad; the food was actually pretty good), and most recently, a Chinese food restaurant has opened at that location. Wonder if French food will be next!

The problem with this "ideal" location is that the access is terrible. The property has great visibility and drive-by traffic, but no one is able to actually stop there and grab a bite to eat very easily.

Residential real estate is the same. Your property should have normal access and be in a normal area. If it is on a super-busy highway, why would a tenant with little children want to rent it and risk their kids running out into a busy street? They won't. Or if the property is in a known drug neighborhood, who is going to want to rent the property from you? Probably other drug dealers!

The concept of centrality comes into play. Is your potential property purchase central or easily accessible to the commuting roads, shopping, schools, churches, family and friends, and your future tenants' job locations?

Future development should also be considered. My wife and I recently purchased several fourplexes in a town of about one hundred thousand people. There was a large vacant lot to the west and to the south of the property. We should research to see what might be built there. If someone is trying to build a drug rehab center or asphalt plant next to our nice, new fourplexes, this will have a major impact on the properties' resellability as well as its rentability. In fact, I did check, and they are building some more fourplexes. Should be a nice community.

Resellability

Attention! This is a real common mistake many people make. You find a property, and lo and behold, the price seems to be significantly below the market. So the offer is made, and the property is purchased. Everything goes well until several years later, when you want to sell the property. Now you must discount the property due to the same reasons the previous owner had to discount it for you to buy it. Some of the reasons could include poor access, bad neighborhood, cracked foundation, etc.

A couple of years ago, I purchased three building lots together in conjunction with a duplex. The duplex has been a great property, and I never paid much attention to the lots because they were so inexpensive to purchase. Now as I consider selling the lots, I have realized that the utilities are not stubbed to the property. In other words, it will cost quite a bit of money to bring the utilities into these lots. Now I know why the original seller was so willing to sell these lots so cheap. And now I, too, will have to discount the lots in order to sell them or be willing to pay to bring in the utilities.

Thus, when you are looking at your potential investment, you must keep in mind that at some point in the future, you, too, will want to sell this property. And any deficiencies will either need to be corrected, or you may need to discount your investment in order to sell it.

Age of the Property

You can make money on new property, slightly used property, and seventy-five-year-old buildings. It is a function of your tolerance for maintenance projects.

New properties are nice in that they have very little maintenance costs or time needed to coordinate maintenance activities. But you may still have yard maintenance, snow removal maintenance, and the inevitable something breaking on the inside, like the garbage disposal. Nevertheless, the costs will be relatively minimal.

Properties newer than twenty-five years old will have a little more maintenance. In addition to the maintenance items of a new property, you will have things such as a new water heater, repainting, new blinds, etc. These maintenance costs will be higher than a new property's.

Properties older than twenty-five years will have all of the above maintenance items and a host of more issues. Some of the major maintenance items will rear their ugly heads, like crack in the foundation, new roof, new furnace/AC unit, major rewiring, major plumbing, etc.

So what is the right strategy in relation to the age of the property? If you like to fix things and are close to the property you intend on buying, then older property is not much of an issue. Or you can have a good handyman or property manager available to repair the property. And the purchase price of older property is almost always less expensive than that of newer property. But under all circumstances, you must plan for major expenditures on older properties during the time you own the property. Getting a thorough home inspection prior to purchase (you can write this into the purchase contract, which we will discuss later) is a must.

If you are not so handy or don't want to be bothered too much with phone calls relating to maintenance, then perhaps newer is the better option for you. You will have some maintenance costs, so again, you must plan this into your cash flow.

Also, keep in mind which properties will rent better. If you were the tenant, would you want to live in a newer property or an older property? Most would, of course, say newer. Thus, the rents on a newer property will generally be higher than on the same-size older property.

HOA/COAs

HOA stands for homeowners' association; COA stands for condominium owners' association. Both function similarly; however, a HOA usually involves single-family homes, whereas a COA typically involves condominium units.

The advantage to owning a property in a HOA/COA is that they will typically have bylaws that require certain things to enhance the value of the property—for example, defining certain types of fencing, exterior appearance, keeping junk off the property, size of structure, etc. By having the neighborhood look well, the value of your property is generally increased.

And some projects will include a number of special amenities, like a community swimming pool, firepits, playground area, etc.

To help cover the costs of administration and maintaining the community items, you will pay a monthly HOA/COA fee. If the project has very few amenities, then the monthly cost will be fairly low. If you have a lot of amenities, the cost can be very high.

Having been in the property management business for many years, I have seen the cost range anywhere from about $25 per month to over $2,500 per month.

Recently, my wife and I purchased a single-family rental home in an average area. One of the attractive aspects of the property was that it wasn't in a HOA; thus, there is no HOA fee. If the HOA fee is too high, it can erode your potential profits on the investment.

You should always verify if the property is in an HOA/COA or not. If it is, ensure that the seller is current on their fees or, at a minimum, you get a reduction in the purchase price equal to the delinquent fees.

Another potential hazard with HOA/COA is, they may periodically have a special assessment. One of our properties was in an area where the Internet connection was very slow. Thus, the HOA decided to bring in high-speed Internet. The consequence was that each household was assessed some $2,600.

You can find great properties that are in or out of a HOA/COA. You just need to understand the fees when you make your offer to purchase the property.

Zoning

What is *zoning*? It's a set of rules created by governments, usually city and county governments, that dictate the types of use a piece of property can have. For example, if a property is zoned for single-family houses only, then you can't build a duplex on the property or convert a single-family house into a duplex.

Thus, it becomes critical to verify all zoning requirements for all your real estate investments. Typical zoning classifications include single-family, multifamily, commercial, agricultural, industrial, and a host of subgroups as well.

Is it possible to change zoning? Sometimes, but it is a process not for the faint of heart! Some requests can literally take years to get completed. And in the end, the rezoning request may be denied.

The average investor should probably steer clear of trying to get zoning changed and keep focused on acquiring investment property that is already zoned for existing rental properties.

A couple of years ago, a friend contacted me and told me they were going through a divorce. Their spouse had already left, and they were stuck with almost a year left on the lease for the house they were renting. The house was an older property that had been converted into a triplex. When I contacted the owner to see how my friend could transition out of the lease, the owner simply said, "Too bad. Keep paying your full rent until the end of the lease."

It seemed a little harsh given the circumstances and the fact that rental properties in that particular area were fairly easy to rent. It didn't quite all add up. So I looked up online the specific zoning for that piece of property, and guess what I found? It was zoned single-family only. After I relayed my findings to the owner of the property, the lease was quickly terminated, and my friend moved.

Do not put yourself in an awkward situation or cause yourself embarrassing or legal problems because you simply didn't verify the zoning of the property you are considering purchasing. And don't get caught up in the "everyone in the neighborhood is doing it" syndrome. Lots of wrongs are not going to make this one right.

Utilities

A number of years ago, I purchased a piece of property that had no utilities, knowing that some-day, I would need to have the utilities brought to the property. When that day came, I was unfortunately surprised at the cost—$15,000. Thus, the real pur-chase price of the lot I had purchased was actually higher than I was anticipating. The return on this investment was decreased.

In buying a property, you should check the source and cost of each of the utilities. Utilities include water, sewer, garbage, electric, natural gas/propane, telephone, and Internet.

Water. Who is the provider, and what is the monthly fee? Does the property have a well? Is the water owned with shares like stock? If so, your offer should include all water shares. Or is the water leased? If so, the lease would need to be transferred to you via the offer. If the property has a little acreage with it, does the seller own enough water to service all of the ground?

For years, my parents and my sister's family lived just outside of Boise, Idaho. Whenever we would drive to visit, we would pass this sign some fifty miles before we arrived that had 240 acres for sale along the interstate. And the price was ridiculously cheap! One day, I asked my brother-in-law if he was familiar with the sign. He said yes, he had seen it many times. I asked him why the property was so inexpensive. As a farmer, his answer was quite simple: "Oh, that piece of property has no water rights." Now I understood why it was so cheap and had been for sale for over twenty years.

In general, if you're buying a rental house within the city limits, the city will be providing the water, and the cost will be nominal.

Sewer. Typically, there will be two possibilities. Either the property is connected to a public sewer system, or the property has a septic tank. If connected to the public sewer, again, the fees typically are nominal per month. If the property has a septic tank, it would be wise to find out when the last time the tank was serviced. If no records are available, then in your offer, you should make the purchase conditional on having an inspection done; replacing a septic tank could cost thousands.

Garbage. If you are purchasing a property in some type of complex, quite often, a large community dumpster is provided. Again, you would want to check the monthly cost and frequency with which the dumpster is emptied. But more often than not, you will have a garbage container provided by a company or city/county that will pick it up once per week. Also, you may have available a recycling container as well. You will want to verify who the service provider is and what the monthly cost will be. Can you imagine owning a property without garbage service? It would be fairly painful to have to take your garbage to the county landfill regularly.

Electricity. In some parts of the country, electricity can be very expensive. Again, you will want to verify the provider and the relative cost of the monthly electric bill. And note that the cost can fluctuate based on seasonality. Thus, you should get the annual cost, which would include all four seasons.

It would be wise to check and see if the heat source (furnace, baseboard heaters, boilers, etc.) and the appliances run off electricity or gas. If they are all electric and electricity is expensive, it will make the property a little more difficult to rent. Thus, you may want to pass on the property or perhaps offer a lower price due to this fact.

My wife and I purchased a nightly rental property once that was only three years old. The neighborhood next door had gas provided, but this newer neighborhood did not. Thus, all the appliances had to be electric. Fortunately, the small electric company that serviced the area provided quality power at a very inexpensive rate. The property is a very profitable rental property.

Gas. Natural gas powers most homes' furnaces, water heaters, and some appliances. It is a relatively inexpensive source of energy. If the property does not have natural gas, then there are generally two alternatives. First, all appliances and heating systems will be electric. You would therefore want to pay close attention to the electricity costs. The second option is to have a large propane tank at the property to provide energy for the furnace, appliances, swimming pool, etc.

Several years ago, we purchased a lot in a subdivision that had no natural gas. We subsequently purchased a large propane tank and had it buried (the HOA actually required it to be buried). So the cost to get a propane tank versus the cost of having everything run off electricity had to be compared. Because we intend to keep this property for the long-term, it will be less expensive to go propane.

Any of these options can work well; you just need to understand how it may affect your profitability.

Telephone. Do people still use landlines? Most don't, but maybe the future buyer of your property does. You will want to check to see if a telephone line has been run to the property.

Internet. Some five years ago, my business partner, Doug, and I decided to purchase a small office building. During the due diligence process, we were informed that there was no Internet to the building. In this modern age, I found it hard to believe that any property, especially an office building, wouldn't have an Internet connection. Due to urgency in wanting to buy this property and move one of our offices into it, we plowed ahead with the purchase.

Some six weeks later, as we were moving one of our companies into the building, we were confronted with the fact that—yes, you guessed it—we had no Internet service. So we contacted a provider and had them rush the service installation. A few thousand dollars later, we had Internet.

In verifying the Internet service for the property you are looking at purchasing, it is important not only to ensure that the service exists but also, additionally, to verify the cost and the speed of the service. Your renters will not be very happy if the Internet is so slow they can't even stream any good *Star Wars* movies.

Summary. Typically, none of the above utility issues will be a deal killer in and of itself. Quite often, they simply become a negotiating tool in acquiring the property. For example, if the property has no Internet, then I simply offer a little less money and will use the savings to bring Internet to the property, if possible. If there is no way to get Internet to the respective property, then I will probably pass on it and look for something else. Note that this due diligence must be completed before we buy the property.

Also, remember that in terms of rental property, the tenant will pay for most of the utility costs. Typically, in a single-family home, the tenant pays for all utilities. In a multiunit property of three or more units, the tenant would usually pay for electric, gas, phone, and Internet. But the property owner (you) would pay the water, sewer, and garbage. In some cases, if the property has separate meters for each of the units for water, that cost can also be passed on to the tenant.

Keep in mind, while the rental property is vacant, you will cover all the utility costs.

Utility Checklist		
	Available (Y/N)	Monthly Cost
Water		
Sewer		
Garbage		

Electric		
Natural Gas/Propane		
Telephone		
Internet		

Maintenance

We will discuss the cost of maintenance in a later chapter. However, it should be a consideration when we purchase the property. For example, we might be looking at a single-family home to purchase as a rental property. It may have immaculate gardens, flower beds, a greenhouse, pools, ponds—wait! Do you think that every one of your tenants through the years will take good care of these things and always have the property looking great? The answer is a resounding no! So if the tenant doesn't, who will? It will either be you overworking on the property every weekend or you will be paying someone to take care of it.

The lesson here is that less is more. A simple lawn with a couple of trees is great. In my thirty-plus years of owning rental properties and managing over one hundred thousand properties, I can assure you that the tenants will rarely pull weeds in the flower beds, and the weeds will not pull themselves out.

Other things to avoid would be wooden fences that need to be painted every other year, flat tar and gravel roofs that will leak occasionally, and a host of other items.

Again, these things are not necessarily deal killers, but they will add to the cost and will thus reduce the returns on these real estate investments.

Neighborhood

What type of neighborhood would you prefer to live in? Does the tenant think any different from you? Probably not. Thus, there are numerous other elements to consider. If the property is on a very busy street, families with small children will probably not want to rent there.

How is the proximity to schools, shopping, churches, hospitals, etc.? And what about access to the job markets? Will the commute to work be too far that it will deter people from wanting to rent the respective property?

And how is the crime rate? Most people will not want to live in a drug-infested neighborhood. So if you buy a property in that type of neighborhood, who will live there? Only drug dealers! That is who your tenant will be. Probably not the best idea even though the property was super cheap.

And what does the future hold for the neighborhood? Recently, our son and daughter-in-law purchased a new home in a new neighborhood. The property seemed to be priced average. But over the past year, building has increased in the area significantly, numerous high-tech businesses have come to the area, and they just broke ground for a major new hospital a few blocks away. This property has gained some 30 percent appreciation in just over a year!

Appreciation

One of the great benefits of real estate is that it continues to increase in value over time. From cave-person times, through the ages, down to now, real estate has continued to increase in value. Yes, there have been many peaks and valleys, but the six-thousand-year trends look very impressive.

Here is a graph showing the increase in value of real estate from 1951 to 2021.

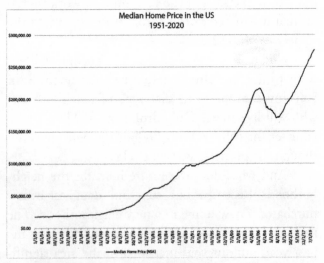

The National Association of Realtors, the Federal Housing Finance Agency, Robert Shiller, and the US Bureau of Labor Statistics. December 16, 2020.

Many of the items above that we have discussed can have an impact on the future increase in value of the property. And there are several other factors that can help. For example, a smaller house in a neighborhood that has larger houses will usually be pulled up in value. The reason is, people like to live in the "bigger house" neighborhood but not have to pay the full "bigger house" price.

The inverse is equally true. If you buy the biggest house in the neighborhood, the smaller homes' prices will tend to pull your home's price down a little bit.

Think of it this way: If I bought a fifteen-thousand-square-foot Bel Air mansion and moved it to a ghetto in a large city, surrounded by one-hundred-year-old shacks, what would happen to the mansion's value? Could I sell the mansion for as much or more in the ghetto versus California? I don't think so.

During the COVID-19 pandemic, many people were moving from heavily populated areas like New York and San Francisco to less-populated areas such as Idaho. The appreciation on properties in Idaho has been incredible.

You will want to look for properties that have a strong upside for appreciation. After all the money you make while owning the property, you get a big bonus when you sell the property if it has appreciated significantly.

In summary, there are a lot of things to consider in finding the right property. Also, please note that the perfect investment property does not exist.

If it did, everyone else would have already purchased it, and there still wouldn't be the perfect property. Therefore, there must be some give-and-take. For example, if the property doesn't have natural gas, then the electric bill will be somewhat higher. I can offer to buy it for a little bit less, knowing that the power costs will be a little bit higher, and most of that cost will be passed on to the tenant. This will not stop me from purchasing the property if everything else is in line.

It has been my experience over the past thirty-plus years that as long as you buy correctly on the front end, you will almost always come out well on the back end. In other words, if you pay too much or the property has too many issues, it is difficult to make good money during the ownership period and again when you sell it.

In all the real estate deals I have been a part of, I can only remember one that didn't make really good money. Many years ago in Utah, I purchased two mobile homes for a great price—I thought. Within one week of having purchased the properties, I received a letter from an attorney representing the mobile home park informing me that the park had been sold and that the new owners wanted my mobile homes removed within five days—yes, five days! After checking with my attorneys, I learned that I did, indeed, have to move my mobile homes. Why hadn't I spoken with the mobile home park owners to understand what was in store for the future of the park that could affect my properties?

I called every mobile home park in the area, but not a single one would take my mobile homes. The parks were reserving their lots to build and sell manufactured homes, a far more profitable venture for them than collecting a lot fee from me every month.

After an exhaustive search, I finally found a mobile home park that would take my homes—in Wyoming! So we had them torn down and shipped them to Evanston, Wyoming (for an additional several thousand dollars). Well, the end of the story is, things didn't go that well, and I ended up selling both units and carrying a contract on them. After two years of pain, I made about $100 on the deal.

So here is the real lesson: If you buy right, you will almost always come out right. And you must do your homework/due diligence on the front end. It will not help you to learn about the problems after you have purchased the property. If so, you will get to literally pay for the problems, either in real money or in reduced rental income and/or reduced resale price.

≡ CHAPTER 5 ≡

Where to Find the Right Property

Now that we have an idea of what to look for in a rental property, we must figure out where to find it. In 2019, there were over six million homes sold in the US. Plus there were over 250,000 multiunit (more than four units in the building) that sold that year as well. And of course, a host of duplexes, triplexes, and fourplexes was purchased.

There are literally millions of buyers looking for property. Therefore, it is important to know where to look and how to look. Otherwise, you will only be able to find the less-than-desirable properties at a less-than-desirable price.

Before you start looking, you should select two or three areas where you are comfortable owning property. If you think you will self-manage the property, then you should not go beyond about forty-five minutes from where you live. If the property is farther away, you will soon be regretting the drive to fix things or show the property to a potential renter.

If you are going to use a property management company, it is true that your monthly operating costs, in the form of a management fee, will be a little bit higher. But it will also allow you to buy properties where the best deals exist versus buying one just because it is close. Believe it or not, most of the great deals are probably not just in your neighborhood.

Let's take a look at several sources to find rental properties.

Internet

The Internet is the first obvious choice. There are some great websites that can give you access to thousands of properties for free. Some of these include Realtor.com, Zillow.com, Craigslist.com, Trulia.com, FSBO.com (For Sale by Owner), Loopnet.com, etc. Most of these sites will list thousands of properties for sale in all fifty states. Thus, you can find properties right in your neighborhood or across the country.

So the good news is, there are lots of options to look at. But the bad news is that thousands of buyers just like you have access to the same information at the same time as you do. Therefore, the great deals that come up are sold within hours, not days or months.

I recently found a home for sale that had been on one of these sites for less than twelve hours. The price looked pretty good, and the property itself looked great, right in the neighborhood I was looking. We liked the property enough that we decided to call the agent and make the offer over the phone without even seeing the property.

I called the agent around eight o'clock the next morning. To my surprise, they had already received six offers, and the owner accepted the best one—too late.

Continuing to look at these sites is a good idea. You may find a great deal and can act on it. Also, it will help you become familiar with various markets and the current prices in that particular location.

Real Estate Agents

Another good source of properties are real estate agents. In a typical situation, an agent is contacted by someone who wants to sell their property. The seller signs an agreement to have the agent market and sell the property. Once the agreement is signed, then the agent puts a For Sale sign on the property, perhaps holds open houses, and lists the property on the multiple listing service (MLS) in their area. Once on the MLS, the home will typically show up on most of the Internet sites listed above as well. So that puts us back where we were: listed home on Realtor.com/Zillow/ etc., where thousands of people can see it.

But what about the person who contacts an agent and isn't sure if they want to sell their property? Or what about the person the agent has worked with in the past who has considered selling but hasn't committed yet? Or the seller who is always open to selling for the right situation?

A couple of years ago, I was talking with an agent I had known for many years. He casually mentioned to me he knew of an owner that lived in a different state that might consider selling her nine duplexes. I immediately said, "When can we go see them?" Note that the owner hadn't even decided whether or not to sell the units. A couple of days later, Doug and I and the agent scheduled a time and went to look at the units.

The units were a little older than we would normally purchase, but they were in pretty good condition and were fully rented (though the rents were too low). Within a day, we came up with a price we were willing to pay. The agent reached out to the owner with our offer, even though the units were not for sale. After going back and forth on price a couple of times, we came to an agreement. We bought the properties even though they were not for sale! And best of all, we did not have to compete with thousands of "eyes" looking at the listing on the Internet.

Agents know lots of owners/investors and can be a great source of off-market properties for sale. I would guess more than 50 percent of all the properties we have purchased were off-market.

Other Sources

There are numerous other sources to find off-market properties. Many of the larger construction companies will not list their properties with an agent and, subsequently, are not on the traditional sales websites. They do this to avoid having to pay up to a 6 percent commission to an agent. They, in turn, market the properties themselves via their company websites and usually have a model home that you can walk through. One of my sons and his wife recently purchased a home in this fashion—saved some pretty good money—and will shortly turn this into a rental property.

Some other sources include family members, friends, neighbors, work associates, school associates, church associates, etc. Your ears should always be listening for someone to mention that "a friend is thinking of moving." It is so easy to simply inquire as to the situation and perhaps find a great deal. Several years ago, I had a fellow coworker comment that a relative had passed away and they just wanted to get rid of the property as is. It didn't take long until we had an agreement in place to buy the property.

There are a host of other sources as well. No one knows more about a rental property and how it performs than the property manager. They hear from owners frequently about selling their property. It would be wise to work with some good property managers to find off-market properties.

There are also wholesalers that will buy and then resell to investors like you. There are a number of companies across the country that provide this service. You can also go to county records and obtain the mailing address of most anyone that owns a particular property, as it is all public information. I recently received a letter from an individual that indicated they wanted to know if I would sell a recreational lot that we purchased just six months ago; they got my name from the county records.

There are foreclosures, auctions, mailing lists, and a host of other sources. With a little effort and the Internet, you *can* find off-market properties for sale.

Okay, so what have we learned about finding the right properties to purchase? First, you can go to the primary Internet sites and see thousands of properties, knowing every other investor in the country can see them as well. So if you find one, you must act quickly to purchase.

Second, most of the better deals are found off-market through various means. Always keep your eyes and ears alert for properties that might make sense to purchase.

Here is your first assignment: Pick three markets where you might have an interest in purchasing a property. They don't need to be close together or even in the same state. Then each day, jump on Realtor.com and Zillow.com and look at properties for sale in those three markets. This will take maybe ten minutes a day. Let's start simple by looking only for single-family homes. Both of these websites have filters, so you can request single-family homes only.

Typically, the best configuration for a single-family house rental property is four bedrooms and two bathrooms. If it has more bathrooms, that is a little bonus. More bedrooms typically will increase the price of the property but not necessarily get you more rent per month to cover the increased cost of the property. Likewise, a two-bedroom house is almost too unique, and you generally won't get the respective rent from the property for the purchase price of the home. A three-bedroom home can work, but generally not as good a return on your investment versus a four-bedroom home.

So for your assignment, let's only look at four-bedroom and two-bathroom homes. Again, you can filter the search fields this way. As you look at the properties, you should also note the purchase price of the property and the cost per square foot. These will both guide you in evaluating the properties correctly. Get quite focused on an area that has maybe ten-plus listings. You can click the "Map View" to hone in on a particular neighborhood.

Do this exercise for ten days. After this short amount of time, you will become a pricing expert for that particular area. You will start to see properties that seem abnormally high, and you will see properties that seem abnormally low. Of course, the high ones, we avoid. The low ones need an explanation, of which only two exist: either there is something wrong with the property, or it is a good deal and it's time to purchase.

So what kind of things can be "wrong" with the property? The property is on a busy street, roof has holes in it, the IRS has tax liens against the property, no gas service and electricity is very expensive, etc.

It should be noted that there are many homes outside of the four-bedroom, two-bath configuration that can work. There are always good deals at every level and bad deals at every level. But for the purpose of this assignment, stick with one configuration. You will amaze yourself at how quickly you will become a market expert on homes for sale in those three neighborhoods you've chosen. Don't wait; start today! It costs nothing except ten minutes a day for ten days.

≡ CHAPTER 6 ≡

Money to Do the Deal

There are numerous sources to pay for the real estate you want to purchase. Let's take a look at some of the sources.

Cash

Cash is the most obvious. Some of the advantages in using cash is that you can get the transaction done quickly and often negotiate a better purchase price. Also, you will avoid all the lender fees, such as loan origination (typically 0.5 percent to 2 percent of the loan amount), appraisal fees, etc. These transactions are cleaner; however, if you have limited amounts of cash, spending it all on one deal may preclude you from doing more deals, perhaps even better deals than the one that you are doing. But there is some peace of mind knowing that you don't have a mortgage payment.

Traditional Lenders

Because most of us don't always have a few hundred thousand in cash lying around, borrowing becomes important. Traditional lenders would primarily include banks and credit unions. They will require you to demonstrate you have income to support your purchase via tax returns and paystubs. The lenders will also require an appraisal to ensure the property is worth what they are going to loan you for the purchase. We will cover specific terms of lending in the next chapter.

Hard Money

This is simply a loan from a nontraditional source. This type of loan is generally easier to qualify for, but the fees/interest rate will be higher than a traditional lender. Also, these loans are rarely long-term loans. For example, you may procure a hard-money loan for one year, which allows you to purchase the property. But by the end of twelve months, you will need to refinance the property to pay off the hard-money loan. The terms of these loans are open for negotiation, which includes the interest rate, loan origination fee, and length of the loan.

Seller Financing

Seller financing is when the seller essentially becomes the lender. You pay a down payment and then start making mortgage payments to the seller. This is a great way to purchase a property. A few years ago, I saw a property that I wanted to buy. But at that time, we were purchasing a number of different things, and I didn't want to tie up any cash on this particular property. As I read through the listing, it mentioned the seller might consider financing part of the deal. I quickly submitted the offer of 10 percent down, with the balance being paid over five years at 5 percent interest. The owner responded that he would accept the deal if the interest rate were 6 percent. We signed the deal and purchased the property, having only needed some $30,000 down. So why don't we see more seller-financed deals? Most sellers want all their money when the property closes, or they have a loan on the property that will probably need to be paid off.

1031 Exchange Money

This, 1031, refers to the section of the Internal Revenue Service (IRS) Code that deals with trading or exchanging property. Basically, this section allows you to sell a property, take the money from the sale, and reinvest it in a different property without having to pay any tax on the gain from the original sale. This is a great method to build up your portfolio of properties. We will discuss 1031 exchanges in more depth in chapter 8.

Home Equity Loan

This is where you would get a home equity loan on the current home that you live in and then use some of the loan proceeds to purchase a rental property. This can be an effective way to get started, assuming you have equity in your home. Over the past ten years or so, most homes have appreciated significantly, and there is a good chance you have equity. Like all options, there are some risks here. For example, if you borrow against the house you live in and then purchase a rental, your debt level has increased substantially. That is okay, unless something goes really wrong, like you losing your job and the rental property can't be rented for some reason. Then you run the risk of losing both the rental property and your home.

Miscellaneous Sources

There are still many other options for sources of capital to purchase real estate. Some would include a self-directed IRA, borrowing against a 401(k) or other retirement fund, borrowing against a life insurance policy, credit cards, family, friends, etc. As you look into these options, you would want to consult a professional as other aspects of your life may get disrupted if things do not go well (borrowing money from Grandma and then not paying her back makes for difficult family reunions).

Co-ownership

Sometimes, there just isn't a way to pull together all the funds by yourself to do a deal. Perhaps finding a partner is the right approach for you. Let's assume you were looking at purchasing a $300,000 duplex. Normally, you would need 25 percent down, which would be $75,000, and you would need to qualify to borrow the difference of $225,000. If you had one equal partner, then everything is cut in half: only $37,500 down and qualify to borrow $112,500. This will be much easier. Or if you had three partners, you would only need to have $18,750 down and qualify to borrow $56,250; that's doable! Of course, then only 25 percent of the profits come your way, but at least you got the deal done and you are making some money.

Over half of all the properties we have purchased through the years have been with a partner. It makes it easier to get into various real estate deals, even though the returns are reduced by the number of partners. So then you just do more deals.

Be wise in selecting partners. They need to have financial stability and be able to execute on the plans when the time comes to finalize the purchase. If not, you may get left in a situation that you cannot afford. Also, note that in dealing with family members and good friends, if someone doesn't follow through on their commitments, the deal goes bad, along with the relationship.

Lease-Option

A *lease-option* is an agreement in which the landlord/owner and tenant agree that at the end of a specified period, the renter can buy the property. The tenant usually pays an up-front option fee and an additional amount each month that goes toward the eventual down payment. For example, let's assume that the tenant (you) paid $1,000 up front, plus an extra $250 per month toward the purchase. At the end of twelve months, you would have paid $1,000 + $250 × 12 months = $4,000 toward a down payment. Note that if you do not follow through and buy the property per the terms of the agreement, your money is typically forfeited. This can be a way to acquire a property when cash is scarce on the front end of a transaction. But remember, you still need to be able to qualify for a loan by the end of the option period, typically one to three years later.

Options

An *option agreement* is where you pay some up-front money for the right to acquire a specific property by a certain date. For example, maybe there is some ground that you would like to purchase so that you can build a duplex on the property. However, the ground is not zoned for duplexes even though there are several duplexes near the property. You might "option" the property contingent upon being able to get the property rezoned for a duplex.

The option prevents the seller from selling the property to someone else until your option expires or you actually buy the property. The option money is not refundable but can be applied toward the purchase typically.

≡ CHAPTER 7 ≡

Lending/Borrowing Terms

Most investors, like yourself, will borrow money to purchase their real estate. Understanding the basics of financing will help you get deals done profitably. Understanding how lending works not only can make or break a deal but also, with incorrect borrowing, can cost you lots of money and turn a good deal into a not-so-good deal. So let's look at the components of a traditional loan.

Down Payment

We use this term frequently. It refers to the amount of cash you will have to pay when you close on the property. This amount is primarily set by the lender. If you are buying a home to live in, the amount will be somewhere between 3 percent and 5 percent down. So if you are buying a $400,000 home, you will need $12,000 to $20,000 down.

If you are buying an investment property, you will need some 25 percent down. Thus, if you are buying a $400,000 fourplex, you will need $100,000 down. Lenders view rental properties as a little riskier than loaning money for an owner-occupied house. This is because people are far less likely to stop paying their mortgage on the home where they live versus a rental property that is just an investment.

Interest Rates

Currently (2021), mortgage interest rates are at historic lows. You can get a thirty-year mortgage at around 2.625 percent for a home that you are going to live in. Interest rates for investment properties will be slightly higher, again due to the perceived increased risk by the lender. Investment property interest rates will be one half of a percent to three-fourths of 1 percent higher. So if owner-occupied rates are at 2.625 percent, then investment property rates would be around 3.125 percent to 3.375 percent. These rates are amazingly cheap! This will help your property generate positive cash flow even after the mortgage has been paid!

There are also different kinds of rates in addition to the rate itself. Most loans are a *fixed rate*—meaning, the rate will stay the same for the duration of the loan period.

There are also *variable rates*, which means that the rate can move up or down, depending on the economy. These rates usually start out a little lower than a fixed rate, but you have the possibility that the rate can increase above what the fixed rate would have been. This could happen if the economy gets really strong and the Federal Reserve increases rates to slow borrowing and thus "cool down" the economy. The reverse could be true as well, that the economy is too cool and the Feds want to stimulate growth via borrowing. Then they could reduce the borrowing rates, and your mortgage interest rate would decrease.

So when would you do a variable rate versus a fixed rate? If I was planning on selling the property in a shorter time frame, I might take the lower variable rate and sell the property before the rate increases. Thus, I save hundreds, or perhaps thousands, of dollars in interest payments. The risk is that the rate suddenly increases. However, even in those cases, the rate is usually capped around a maximum of 2 percent increase above the initial rate. So if I started at 3.125 percent, the rate could never exceed 5.125 percent.

Lenders will sometimes offer you the opportunity to "buy down" the interest rate. Essentially, you prepay some of the interest when you purchase the property (increasing total amount of money you will need at closing). In return, the interest rate will be reduced. So which is best? It depends on your strategy for the property. If you are going to acquire and then sell the property fairly quickly, then there is no need to prepay any of the interest for a "buy-down" (no one is going to refund you any interest for selling early). If you are going to keep the property long-term, buying down the interest rate can make some sense. This is a simple mathematical calculation to see how many years/months you would need to own the property to benefit from buying down the interest rate—how much money in prepaid interest was paid versus how much interest I will save every month on the mortgage payments. Typically, five to six years is normal to reach breakeven. In other words, you will come out ahead if you don't buy down the rate and sell the property less than the five years or so. Or if you are keeping the property longer than five years, it probably makes sense to buy down the interest.

On occasion, it can make sense to do an interest-only loan. Usually, this is used on a short-term basis, when cash flow is tight. You will need to either sell the property and pay off the loan or put a more permanent long-term loan in place at a future date.

Loan Origination Fee/Points

Most traditional lenders will have a fee called loan origination or points. This fee is simply an amount the lender may charge you so they can make more money (which means you make less money). It can vary from as high as 2 percent down to nothing. A typical fee charged would be 1 percent. If you are borrowing, let's say, $300,000, then this fee would be 1 percent × $300,000 = $3,000, which will be added to your closing costs. Yes, you are paying $3,000 for the privilege of borrowing their money. Don't! This fee is definitely negotiable. If the lender won't drop or reduce it next to nothing, then it's time to find a new lender. This is just another way the lender makes more money. I have not paid a loan origination fee in over ten years, and I don't see it happening in the next ten either.

Term

The word *term* refers to the length of the loan. There are many options. The most common would be a thirty-year mortgage. But with investment property loans, we see five-, ten-, fifteen-, twenty-, twenty-five-, thirty-, and forty-year lengths for mortgages. The longer the term is on your loan, the lower the monthly payment will be. That's the good news. But also, the longer the term, the more interest you will pay on the total loan. You should also note that if you can do a shorter term—say, fifteen years—quite often, the interest rate is a little bit less than that of a thirty-year loan. Thus, you will pay a lot less interest, and the property will have no debt in fifteen years if you simply pay the minimum payment each month.

Balloon Payment or Call

Some loans will allow you to pay a low monthly payment for a specified period, like five years. But the low monthly payment will not be enough to pay off the loan in the five years. So at the end of five years, you will have to pay off the entire balance. This type of a loan helps you get into or buy the property, but you will either have to come up with the remaining balance in five years or get a new loan to pay off the balance or balloon payment. The term *call* simply means the loan has a time limit and the lender can ask for the balance of or "call" the loan due. Again, you will need to plan and have the cash available or plan to have a new loan in place to pay off the balance on the loan. Sometimes, the same lender holding the call option or balloon will be willing to provide the new long-term loan to replace the original loan.

Reset

Some loans have a reset clause. This allows the lender to "reset" the interest rate. It protects the lender if rates are going up, then they can raise your rate a specified amount so that they stay more current with market rates. Thus, the lender's risk is reduced. So how does this help you? The initial rate may be a little bit lower because the lender's risk is a little bit lower. Also, if you are planning to sell the property within the reset period, then the reset is irrelevant. Or if rates do not increase, then this has no impact on you.

Appraisal

How do appraisals affect borrowing? Once the bank has basically approved your financial ability to pay back the loan as the borrower, it needs to approve the property. This simply means that the property is worth what the bank is loaning against it. And sometimes, they may even require some maintenance be done to the property. The lender is all about protecting their investment in the loan they give you. If, for whatever reason, they have to take back the property in lieu of you paying the loan, the lender needs to ensure they can sell the property for more than the loan granted and get all their money back.

So the lender will send out an appraiser to determine the value of the property. This will cost some $500, which will be charged back to you. As long as the appraisal comes in near or greater than the cost of your offer to the seller, everything is a go. If the appraisal comes in lower, then the lender will lend a lesser amount. This means you either can't do the deal or you will need to come up with more down payment if you still want to pursue purchasing the property. Note that the offer you make is typically contingent on you getting financing and the property appraising for the asking price. So if the property doesn't appraise high enough or you don't qualify for a loan, you will get your earnest money refunded to you.

Closing Costs

Closing costs can vary among title companies and also vary in different parts of the country. Some common costs you will pay as a buyer are prorated property tax, HOA fee prorations, closing fee to the title company, recording fee, and of course, the amount of the purchase, including any borrowing costs. Closing costs for the seller include prorated property tax, HOA-fee prorations, real estate agent commissions, title insurance policy (this is insurance that provides for the title to be clear of encumbrances), and closing fee to title company. Most of these fees are fairly nominal in relation to the price of the property and the sales commissions, if any. The above is fairly standard, with the title company's fee usually being split fifty-fifty.

Review the closing statements before you get to closing, or, if signing online, review before you sign. Quite often, a fee will sneak into the documents. Two years ago, I was closing on a condo that we were selling. As we were in the title company's office signing documents, I noticed that there was some fee called broker fee. When I asked what that fee was, the response was that it was standard. Having been a broker myself for over twenty-five years, I wasn't sure what additional service I was paying for or to whom that $250 was going to be paid. (I actually assumed it was just another way the real estate office was trying to get some more money from me.) There were already two real estate brokerages that were getting commissions, and this was the first time I had seen this on the documents. After they encouraged me to just sign the documents, I politely declined and stood up and left the room. The escrow agent followed me and asked, "Are you really not going to close?" I politely said, "That is correct. The terms have been changed, and I did not agree to the changes."

She seemed somewhat put out but asked me if I would sign if they eliminated that fee. I said of course, I would because that was what had been agreed to previously. We subsequently went back into the room, the escrow agent went to reprint the documents without the broker fee, and we closed the sale. The seven minutes to review and question the fee was worth saving $250. Don't be pushed around. If you see something outside of the normal, you should question it, and remember, almost everything is negotiable.

In the closing process, you can usually select the title company to use. Be sure to establish a good, long-term working relationship with a title company (more about this later). They can be your ally and save you lots of time and money. A title company I used frequently once saved me over $20,000 from an error the seller's title company had made.

If you own a rental property and have a loan on the respective property, will that affect you getting a second loan to buy the second property? Yes. But it can actually help you borrow or reduce your ability to borrow, depending on the rental property's profitability. For example, let's assume you own a fourplex that rents for $5,000 per month, and you have a mortgage for $3,100 on the property. Your net profit would be $1,900. The lender, in order to calculate your income, will subtract 25 percent of the gross income from the rental property due to possible vacancy and other items. Thus, instead of $1,900 of income per month being calculated to determine your borrowing ability, they will take the $5,000 of income less 25 percent and then subtract your mortgage: $5,000 × 25 percent = $1,250; then $1,900 – $1,250 = $650. Thus, the lender will count $650 to you as income in qualifying for the second loan.

Let's assume the same example above, except that the fourplex only rents for $4,000 per month.

If we subtract 25 percent ($4,000 × 25 percent = $1,000) from the gross income of $4,000, we get $3,000. Then $3,000 less the mortgage payment of $3,100 is minus $100. In this case, the lender will subtract $100 from your other income, which will actually reduce the amount you can borrow for the second loan/property.

So what are the basics in qualifying for a loan? First would be to have a good credit score. Currently, a score of 630 or higher will help you qualify. But having a FICO score of over 700 will help get you the better rates/terms. The lower your score, the greater credit risk you are; thus the higher rates will be assessed. You can review your credit score once per year for free by going to annualcreditreport.com.

Secondly, your debt ratios will come into play. There are many variables and exceptions. But to boil it down very simply, your total monthly bills (debts) divided by your gross monthly income should not exceed 45 percent. Let's assume your monthly gross income is $6,000 per month. Let's also assume that you have a car loan of $300 per month, furniture loan of $200 per month, and the new mortgage of $2,000 per month—which, added together, would equal $2,500 per month. Then $2,500 divided by $6,000 equals 42 percent. Because 42 percent is just under 45 percent, you would just barely qualify for this loan of some $330,000.

So are you ready for an assignment? Your assignment is to go to a lender and get prequalified for a loan. That way, you know how much you are able to borrow. Nothing worse than making/receiving an offer only to learn two months later that the lender will not loan the money, and so the deal is dead, wasting everyone's time.

Once you know how much a lender will loan you, then you know what your limits are on the purchase price of properties. In other words, if you qualify for a $300,000, then don't waste your time looking to buy a $500,000 property.

Your next assignment is to purchase a financial calculator application for your phone. I like the HP12C (it cost $11.95), but there are hundreds of easy-to-use apps, many of which are free. These simple apps can calculate payments instantly or help you estimate values and interest costs. These calculations are easy to do and will help you make more informed decisions. Note that we buy real estate investments based on numbers and returns on our investments, not on gut feel or the color of paint in the bathroom. Thus, a financial calculator is important.

CHAPTER 8

Real Estate and Taxes

Do we dare say that Uncle Sam can be our friend? Maybe not, but there are great tax advantages in owning real estate. Let's first understand what type of taxes we are talking about as there are many types.

The primary tax we will explore is income tax, which we will come back to in a minute. Other taxes include property tax and employment taxes. Most states have property tax, which is typically paid once per year. The amount ranges widely based on the value of the property and the tax rate for the respective state/county/city. Often, about 1 percent of the county-assessed value is charged for property tax.

Employment taxes would include social security, unemployment taxes, and self-employment taxes. The good news is that both your rental income from the property and the gain on a sale of your real estate are generally not subject to employment taxes.

So let's explore income tax. This is the tax that you would pay the IRS and your state (a few states have no income tax) on the income you earn. Your rental income is subject to this tax. So the rents for the year less all expenses would give you your net income or profit. That amount will be subject to income tax.

For example, let's suppose you had a rental house and it rented for $1,500 per month or $18,000 per year. Let's also assume that you had expenses of $2,000 in property tax, $1,000 in insurance, $1,200 in maintenance costs; and $1,400 in utility expenses. If we add up all the costs, that would equal $5,600 in annual expenses. Our $18,000 of rental income less the annual costs of $5,600 would give us a net profit of $12,400. This amount would be subject to income tax.

But wait! What about depreciation? Currently, the tax code allows us to depreciate residential real estate over 27.5 years and commercial real estate over 39 years. So in our example, let's assume that we paid $250,000 for the property. Also note that the land portion of the cost of real estate is not deductible. If $40,000 is the value of the land, then we could depreciate $250,000 less $40,000, divided by 27.5 years (250,000 − 40,000 = 210,000 ÷ 27.5 = $7,636). What does this mean? I get a $7,636 tax deduction for the next 27.5 years or until I sell the property. That is amazing!

So in our example, my $12,400 of profit is offset by a depreciation of $7,736; thus, the only amount that is actually taxed is $12,400, less $7,736, which is $4,763. Most of the income is sheltered from taxes thanks to depreciation.

Your rental property is somewhat like owning a small business. And everything going into your "business" is tax-deductible. Some examples may include the laptop that you do the accounting on, your printer at home, your mileage driving to inspect the property (currently deductible at fifty-eight cents per mile), the lawn mower you purchased to take care of the lawn, etc.

As your rental portfolio grows over time, you should look for legitimate ways to turn your life's expenses into a tax deduction. These deductions will help bring your taxable income down, saving you thousands of dollars in taxes and earning you greater returns on your real estate investments.

The example used above assumed the property in question had no mortgage payment. If you have borrowed money to buy the property (which mostly all people do), then you would have a mortgage payment. The interest amount of the payment is also tax-deductible. However, the principal amount is not tax-deductible; that is one reason you get to depreciate the building. Thus, taxable income would be lowered by the amount of interest payments. And the actual cash you receive would also be lowered by the amount of the mortgage payment. We will take a little deeper dive into this later when we look at analyzing a property for purchase consideration.

A second type of income you have with real estate is the profit when you sell the property (I'm assuming you are not going to sell the property for a loss!). For example, if you purchased a property for $300,000 then sold it for $400,000 two years later, you would have a profit of $100,000. This profit is taxed more favorably! Because you have held the property for more than a year, this profit or gain is considered a capital gain. Capital gains are taxed at lower rates than ordinary income. Currently, the tax rates range from 0 to 20 percent, depending on your total income.

Current capital gain tax rates based on your income in 2020:

- $53,600 or less, you pay zero.
- $53,601–$469,050, you pay 15 percent.
- Over $469,051, you pay 20 percent.

This is essentially half of ordinary income tax rates! Don't you wish most of your income came from capital gains? Maybe you need to get even more serious about becoming a real estate investor.

Quite often, we hear the term *exchange* or *1031 exchange*. This refers to the section of Internal Revenue Code 1031, which provides the ability to sell your property, take the gains or profits, and use them to buy another property or properties without paying any tax. Yes, without paying any tax.

Recently, I sold for $260,000 a property that I purchased two years earlier. The purchase price two years ago was $175,000. Thus, the gain was about $85,000, and the tax due on the gain would be about $17,500 to IRS and about $4,000 for state income tax. But I put the property into a 1031 exchange, and so I will pay no tax, saving $21,500! I can now use this savings to help buy another property.

So what are the rules concerning these exchanges? Prior to the sale of your property, you want to note in the offer/acceptance of your real estate transaction that you are potentially going to do a 1031 exchange. Secondly, you will want to contact a reputable company that does 1031 exchanges. Your title company can probably refer one to you. When you close on your property, the 1031 exchange company will have you sign some documents that will qualify the property to be considered a bona fide 1031 exchange.

For the property to qualify for an exchange, you must have owned it for more than one year. Once you have closed, you have exactly forty-five days to identify some properties that you are interested in purchasing. If you miss this deadline, you will not be doing an exchange, and your gain will be taxable.

So think ahead. You should be looking for the new property or properties before you sell. It does you no good to sell a property for a nice gain and then turn around and overpay for a new property, giving up all your gain. You might as well keep the gain, pay the tax, and move on versus buy an over-priced property.

In the property that I sold recently, I had already made an offer on a new property but didn't close on the new property I was buying until after I sold the prior property for $260,000. Thus, it was easy to identify the property I was buying within the for-ty-five days.

Also, after you have identified the properties, you must close on them within 180 days. If you do not, then your exchange will be undone, and you will pay the tax on the gain.

Relax! This process is simple. Your 1031 exchange company will easily guide you through this process. When you sell, the monies from the sale actually go to the exchange company, and they hold them until you purchase the new property. Then they send the money to the title company to purchase the new property. If the new property doesn't require all the money—in other words, if I had bought a new property for $250,000 but had $260,000 in the exchange—then I would receive the excess $10,000 and be taxed on only that amount.

Take note: this is a great way to build wealth, by not paying taxes on your real estate gains and then using those savings to purchase more real estate. There is currently no limit to the number of transactions you can do.

With real estate, avoiding taxes is quite easy (and legal, of course) and can help you build substantial sums of wealth. You should consult a qualified CPA/accountant in these tax matters as tax law changes frequently.

CHAPTER 9

Decision Tools

Recently, a friend called to inform me of a great deal on a rental home that was for sale. After I asked him a couple of questions about the property and I got his answers, I said I would pass on the deal, and so should he. I could tell I had burst his bubble, and he still had interest in pursuing buying the property. Based on his answers to the questions, it was clear the property was too expensive and it would be very difficult to get a decent return for his money.

So what questions should we ask? How do we quickly evaluate a property for purchase? Let's take a look at several tools.

1 Percent Rule

This quick tool gives us a simple idea if the property is worth considering. You simply take the asking price of the property and multiply it by 1 percent. This is how much the property should rent for each month. Thus, if we were looking at buying a $400,000 fourplex, then we multiply the purchase price by 1 percent, which would equal $4,000. And how do we know if it will rent for $4,000 per month? Call a local property manager that actually manages property in the same area and ask them how much it would rent for. There are several online rental inquiry companies, but they are just calculated guesstimates for the most part. A reputable property manager in the local area is generally more accurate.

This tool tells us this property would yield 12 percent gross rents on the property. It should also be noted that this tool will quite often skew toward a little older property. That does not mean you should not purchase new. I recently bought several fourplexes that were brand-new.

Cost per Square Foot

This is calculated by taking the purchase price of the property and dividing it by the total square feet. If we use the same example as in the one above and the square footage was 3,600 square feet, then we would calculate $400,000 ÷ 3,600 square feet = $111.11. This means it will cost $111 for each square foot of space in the property.

My friend that called me recently was looking at a property that was three times the cost per square foot in the area. In other words, a typical property in that particular market was running around $125 per square foot; he was looking at one that was about $375 per square foot. The property had great curb appeal, but that deal was never going to work out very well—too expensive!

Pro Forma Income Statement

This is simply building a forecast of how well the property will perform financially. We'll start by estimating the income. This can be done by contacting a local property manager to get an idea of how much the property in question will rent for.

We then create the expected expenses. Property tax is public data and is typically obtainable online from the local county where the property exists. Insurance expense can be obtained from the seller, or you can call a local insurance agent and get an estimate of how much it will cost. If there is a HOA fee, the owner can provide this cost. If you have a mortgage, you can quickly punch into your calculator the loan amount, interest rate, and number of years of the loan to determine the amount of the mortgage. Note that only the interest portion of the loan is actually tax-deductible, but the entire payment will certainly affect your monthly cash flow. All utility expenses can be obtained from the seller, or you can actually call the utility companies to get an estimate of the expected costs. Remember that in many properties, the tenant will pay utilities; thus you may actually pay just a small part or none of the utilities.

Perhaps the most challenging expense to estimate is the cost of maintenance. The newer the property, the lower the maintenance costs will be. The older the property, the more maintenance expenses you will have to pay. Estimate the obvious things first, like mowing the lawn or snow removal if the property is a multiunit and in a cold-climate area. If there are maintenance items you know about—for example, an old roof—then you should estimate some cost to maintain or fix the roof. If not sure of these costs, then use a figure like 6 percent of rents for maintenance. In other words, if the rent is $3,000 per month, then maintenance would be estimated at $3,000 × 6 percent = $180 per month. Here is a simple template that can help guide you in creating your pro forma.

Pro Forma Income Statement			Annual Amounts
Revenues:			
	Rent		$
	Late Fees		
	Utilities		
	Interest		
	Pet Fees		
	Other		
Total Revenues:			$
Expenses:			
	Mortgage Payment		$
	Property Tax		
	Insurance		
	Utility Costs		
		Water	
		Sewer	
		Garbage	
		Gas	
		Power	
	HOA Fees		
	Maintenance Costs		
Total Expenses			$
Net Income/Loss			$

The pro forma income statement will be your most complete way to analyze an investment. This will tell you if the property will make money each month or if you will have to subsidize the property each month. It will also tell you what the return on your investment will be. For example, if a property costs $400,000 and you make $1,000-per-month profit, then $1,000 × 12 months ÷ $400,000 = 3 percent. This would be a weaker investment at just 3 percent return. But if you had a mortgage and you put 25 percent down ($100,000 down), then your return would be $1,000 × 12 months ÷ $100,000 down payment = 12 percent. That deal works. We call this latter calculation the cash-on-cash return. In other words, we calculate the return based solely on the amount of money you actually invested. This is a truer analysis.

But you should also note that the risk is higher as well because you do have a mortgage of $300,000 and the mortgage payment must be paid each and every month.

Cap Rate

The term *cap rate* is used quite often in real estate investing. Even more so when you are referring to returns on commercial property. The cap rate is simply the annual expected profit divided by the purchase price of the property. In our example above in paragraph number 3, the cap rate is the same as the return on the total purchase price—3 percent. This can be a quick way to initially evaluate a property.

However, before offering to buy the property, you would want to create your own pro forma income statement so you have truer costs and thus a truer cap rate.

Comparative M-Ratio

This simple method is used to compare different properties that you are considering purchasing. It will point to the property with the highest return for the money invested. It is calculated by taking the monthly rent divided by the cost per square foot. Let's look at three differing properties, calculate the comparative M ratio, and see which one is best.

Let's assume property A costs $350,000 and is a single-family house of 2,500 square feet. I call a local property manager and learn the property will rent for $2,600 per month. So let's do the math: $350,000 cost ÷ 2,500 square feet = $140. Now let's take the monthly rent of $2,600 ÷ $140 cost per square foot = 18.57.

Let's take property B and assume its cost is $500,000 and it is a fourplex. The monthly rents will be $4,000 per all four units, and the square footage is 4,200. Here is the math: $500,000 cost ÷ 4,200 square feet = $119. Now divide the rents of $4,000 by $119, which equals 33.60.

Property C is a single-family home selling for $300,000. Its square footage is 2,000, and it rents for $2,100 per month. The math is thus: $300,000

÷ 2,000 = $150 cost per square foot. Then $150 divided into $2,100-per-month rent is 14.

Okay, so what have we learned? Simply that property B, even though its purchase price is the highest of the three properties, will be almost twice as productive as property A and C: 33.60 versus 18.57 and 14 respectively. And we also learned that property A will slightly outperform property C. These numbers are not the return on the investments, simply just a quick way to compare multiple properties in their relation to earning income based on the cost of the investment.

None of the above methods take into consideration the amount of appreciation you may receive. That amount is difficult to know, unless you are a fortune-teller or your last name is Nostradamus. Most properties should be evaluated on their existing merits. If you are buying solely based on future appreciation, you need to have a pretty good appetite for risk. Real estate values can change in a matter of days or weeks or months or years. You will need to assess where you think you are in the appreciation cycle and proceed cautiously.

══ CHAPTER 10 ══

Making the Offer

Recently, my wife and I were looking to purchase a house. We had been looking in the area for some time, so we were quite familiar with the types of homes and the values associated with them. Late one afternoon, I saw a property that fit our needs. The size was about right, the area was great, and the price made sense. Later that evening, I showed the property to my wife online. We both agreed that this property was the right one. So I figured I would call them at eight o'clock the next morning, get ahead of anyone else that might be interested in the property, and place an offer on the property.

Like clockwork, I called at eight o'clock the next morning, and the agent, to my surprise, actually answered the phone. I told him we would like to place an offer on the property for the asking price and that we could pay cash so there wouldn't be any contingencies. He kind of chuckled, so I asked him what was so funny. He said that they had received six offers the day before, all of which were cash offers.

Once you have determined the property is right for you, move quickly to get it under contract. Many things can change quickly, like someone else offering first, the seller deciding to not sell the property, the neighbor stopping by and the seller likely selling to their friend, and the list goes on and on.

If you are using a real estate agent to purchase your property, they will usually have a standard form that either the state or real estate group has approved. You should get a blank copy (like right now, go online and get a copy) of the agreement and review it so you are familiar with its various concepts. Most any agent would be happy to review a blank agreement with you so you know what to expect and can move through an offer very quickly when the time comes.

If you are not using an agent, most real estate or contract law attorneys can provide an agreement for you to purchase the property. Don't just hack your way through this one. You want a bona fide document to secure your rights on the property.

Doug, my business partner, and I recently had an agent call us and tell us he had some investors that wanted to purchase an office building that we owned. He indicated that they would close within thirty days. That's pretty quick on a commercial property. So we were intrigued and started to consider selling the building until he told us what they wanted to pay—about 60 percent of its true value. That deal was over fast.

When you are making the offer, don't offer ridiculously low amounts. No one is going to sell their property for a half price. A lowball offer simply makes people mad, and then they would rather not deal with you. If the particular market is a little soft, it is okay to offer less than the listing price. In fact, the higher priced the property is, the more discounted price you can typically offer. Knowing the market and looking at lots of properties will guide you in knowing what market values really are and how much to offer for properties.

Almost as important as the amount of money the buyer is going to receive (and you are going to pay) is how quickly the seller is going to receive the money. Given the choice of getting either $100,000 next year or $95,000 today, most of us would probably take the $95,000 today. Thus, offering to close as quickly as possible is a strong incentive to accept your offer. Generally, depending on the transaction, I like offering to close in twenty days. This is quite quick, and the seller starts mentally spending the money because it is coming soon. It also gives me enough time to do my due diligence to ensure there aren't any major issues with the property.

If the property has been on the market for over three months, the seller may start becoming a little anxious because the property hasn't sold yet. This may provide some extra incentive on the seller's side to accept a little less money. Thus, you have an opportunity to perhaps offer less money and get the deal done.

Also, if the property has some flaws, you can offer less, knowing the flaws will need to be corrected. For example, maybe the bathroom has bright-pink walls. Most tenants wouldn't want pink walls, so you could offer less, explaining that you will need to spend money to repaint the bathroom. There are many flaws that can be discovered to help in justifying a reduction in price.

Another element of making the offer is the earnest money deposit. Note that the earnest money is completely refundable to you if the conditions you have established are not met or if the seller disclosures don't meet your satisfaction. In other words, you can opt out of the deal before these deadlines and get all your money back. A typical earnest money on a residential property might be $1,000; commercial properties would typically be higher, depending on the size of the transaction. So why not offer more money as earnest money to get the seller more motivated to accept your deal?

About a month ago, my business partner, Doug, and I received an offer on an office building we had for sale. We assumed the buyer paid a standard earnest money amount of around $10,000. But no, he had paid $300,000 as earnest money! It is true that if the deal isn't consummated, he will get all his money back. But it also told us that he is serious and he has money. Yes! We accepted his offer.

In your offer, you have the opportunity to set up all types of contingencies. These could include financing being approved, inspections being completed, the subject property appraising for a certain amount, you selling one of your properties first to get the funds to buy the new property, etc. If I receive an offer with twenty-two contingencies, then I am less likely to accept the offer because any one of the twenty-two (or some other number) contingencies could stop the transaction. Thus, making your offer with the least number of contingencies you are comfortable with will generally increase the probability of your offer being accepted.

Timing is important. I once offered to purchase some property verbally, indicating that the following week, I would formalize the offer and send it. The seller agreed to my terms to sell us the property. But over the weekend, the seller's son was in a serious car accident. Because of the accident, the seller decided not to sell the property. Fortunately, the son completely recovered; unfortunately, the seller stayed with their most recent decision and would not sell the property.

Many things can occur that will cause someone to change their mind. When you submit your offer, I would give only two days, maybe three days at most, for them to accept, reject, or counteroffer. This will require them to make a decision quickly, and I can get the property under contract before something disrupts the transaction.

Many people will quibble over small details or small amounts of money. Do not get caught up in dimes when you are dealing in dollars. I once watched a deal go up in flames (not the house) over $400. This was a $400,000 property. That $400 will be meaningless in the grand scheme of getting this property and making some good money.

My wife and I purchased a property a couple of years ago where the furnishings were to be included in the acquisition. When we did the final inspection, the nice flat-screen TV in the master bedroom had been replaced with a much smaller, cheaper TV. We called the realtor, and they spoke with the seller's agent. The message came back to us that the original TV was left in the home. That was definitely not the case. The original TV was probably four years old and worth some $500. We decided to forget it, close the deal anyway, and go buy a much better TV than both of those TVs. It cost us about $900. This property netted over $55,000 last year after all expenses. I can't worry about a $500 old TV that I never received. Had I made the TV an issue and ultimately killed the deal over it, we would be $55,000 poorer this year and the next year and the next year.

In real estate, look for reasons to get the deal done. Go out of your way to be fair and help the seller meet their needs. Life is pretty short, so if you want to be hard-nosed and try to squeeze every penny out of every transaction, you will lose many deals and be somewhat not fun to work with.

CHAPTER 11

Assemble Your Team

As I started to grow the property management company back in the early 2000s, my job title included CEO, sales manager, operations manager, marketing manager, and receptionist (I made our kids be the janitors). Needless to say, it was difficult to be successful at all these positions at the same time. And in fact, there were many people that could perform these various functions far better than I could. For example, I knew a little about marketing, having taken a couple of classes in both undergraduate and graduate school, but there were numerous people that had been trained in marketing and had many years of experience. They were experts, and I was just a warm body trying to keep everything moving forward.

You won't live long enough to become the expert in every aspect of real estate. Thus, you need to surround yourself with your team or supporting cast. Let's take a look at eight of these players, arranged alphabetically.

Accountant

Find a great accountant/CPA that you can trust. But you must also understand their thinking in relation to taxes. Simply taking your financial information and putting it on a tax return correctly is not enough. You want a person that will consult with you, giving you advice on when to invest, how to maximize your deductions, and the timing of transactions to minimize your tax bite.

Much of the tax code has many gray areas in it, along with black-and-white areas. We never cross the black-and-white lines because that is called tax evasion and you go to jail. But you want an accountant that is a little more aggressive in the gray areas that will help you keep taxes to a minimum and thus keep more of your money in your pocket. A good concept is "Aggressive but not greedy."

Attorney

On occasion, some of the real estate transactions get a little complicated. On one occasion, my wife and I sold a house that sat on an acre and a half. The property had two water sources, one for culinary (drinking water) and the other for irrigating/watering the lawn and pasture. About a month after the transaction had closed, I realized that we still owned the water rights to the lawn and pasture. A good attorney would have found this and required that the water rights be transferred as well. Of course, we transferred the water rights to the new owner at no additional cost.

Not just any old attorney or your cousin's stepson's spouse is necessarily a great idea. You want an attorney that has a legal background in real estate and contracts.

Inspector

Rarely will you want to buy a property without having it inspected. Major items like roofs, electricity, plumbing, and foundations can be very costly to repair after you have purchased the property. If you learn about these problems prior to buying, then you can negotiate a better price or pass on the property.

Inspections are not that expensive. You will want to develop a relationship with an inspector that you can trust and they understand the kinds of things you are looking for. In the early years of our investing, I had an inspector go look at a property. After he inspected it, he indicated that several rooms in the house should be painted and the lawn and shrubs should be trimmed. That was a good lesson in restating the obvious, and I got to pay for it—wrong inspector.

Insurance Agent

In 2004, I drove to one of our office buildings only to find there were two big fire engines parked in the parking lot. I walked up to the building to go in the front door, only to be stopped by a fireman. He told me that I could not go in because they were still putting out the fire. It was true! The entire insides of the building had been completely burned up. The only reason it wasn't so obvious from the outside was that it was a cinder block building and the exterior walls seemed to be okay.

I was devastated. Records, files, computers, phone systems, furniture, and everything else in the building were a complete loss. After I cried for five minutes, called my wife, cried for another five minutes, and then called our insurance agent, I could visualize how we were going to survive the fire.

Because we had done lots of business with the agent for many years, she got crews set up immediately to repair the building. They even let our maintenance people do some of the work so we could earn some money on the project. We literally ran a giant phone cord to the property next door (which happened to be vacant, and the owner let us move in rent-free for four months during the fire remodel). That very day, we had a couple of phone lines and one computer backup and processed payroll by 6:00 p.m.

The insurance company was very impressed by how quickly we got our company going again that they gave us a big check for the business continuity in addition to rebuilding the office building in record time.

Knowing your agent well will help you navigate many issues over the years. Typically including your personal items—such as cars, boats, homeowner's insurance, and investment properties—with one insurance company will earn you discounts, and the longer you are with the company, the more additional discounts will be given.

Lender

People like to do business with people they know and can trust. As your lender gets to know you, they will be more inclined to help you figure out ways to get loans done for you. The mortgage industry is heavily regulated, and many things are not very flexible. But knowing a good lender that you can trust and has reasonable fees will help you move quickly in getting deals done. Do not settle for high loan origination fees, high interest rates, or slow loan processing.

Property Manager (The Best)

I might be a little biased here, having been a property manager for over thirty-five years. The property manager is renting, managing, inspecting, and fixing properties every single day. Thus, they understand the local market where you are considering purchasing your investment property. They can provide invaluable information that many websites and aggregators of data simply may not see in your local market or neighborhood.

Some of us will choose to manage our properties by ourselves. That works if you live within about forty-five minutes or less of your property. But if you live farther away or you get a larger portfolio of properties over time, you will want a solid property manager that is smart, knows the markets, and is honest.

Real Estate Agent

The real estate agent can be an extremely valuable resource. My wife and I purchased a property yesterday through an agent. I had called on a property that was listed, but the agent informed me that the property had just been sold. He then asked me if I would be interested in a similar property in the same neighborhood. I said yes, assuming it was priced well. He then proceeded to tell me about the property and that it was going to be listed in about thirty days after the builder finished building the house.

So my wife, Blenda, and I met him at the property a couple of hours later. The house was perfect, brand-new, and actually a little bit larger than the previous house we called on. The price was about $100,000 under the market rate in the area. We made the offer, and it was accepted yesterday!

This agent helped us find a house that was not listed and was at a great price. Because agents meet and talk with so many buyers, sellers, builders, investors, and developers, they quite often are familiar with properties that are not listed or perhaps not even for sale yet. This can be a great resource. Over the past several years, we have purchased many properties this way.

So can there be a downside in using a real estate agent? Sometimes. You simply need to understand their motivation. They earn nothing unless a property closes. Thus, the motivation can be to simply get a deal closed, not necessarily getting you the best price or value. Also, many sellers will add the cost of the real estate commission to the value of the property. For example, if a property is selling for $500,000, a typical real estate commission of 6 percent would be $30,000. The seller may decide to list the price at $530,000 to cover the cost of the commission. This will essentially push the cost of the commission to you as the buyer.

Find several agents you can trust in markets that you are interested in purchasing properties. Each agent will be familiar with different opportunities in addition to what is listed on the MLS (multiple listing service provided by the Board of Realtors). Over the past thirty days, Blenda and I looked at twenty-plus properties with several agents. Agent D's property was sold, but she showed us a great property that was about fourteen days away from being listed. Agent T's property was also sold, but he showed us one that we purchased. Agent B showed us a property that was also going to be listed in about two weeks, which we did not buy. But his partner showed us some building lots that were going to be available in about sixty days; we tied one of them up.

So after spending time with a number of agents, we purchased two properties that we heard about from real estate agents and were great deals and were not listed for sale. You can do it! Call some agents and get looking today.

Title/Escrow Company or Real Estate Attorney

Using these companies is how you can sleep at night, not having to worry about monies getting transferred correctly at sale or actually getting "ownership" or title to the property. Most states use title or escrow companies to close real estate transactions. However, a handful of states, mostly in southern US, use attorneys to close transactions. Having a good company ensures the transaction happens correctly (you are still responsible to make sure it is a good transaction to begin with). The title company's role is to act as a third party by sending the buyer's money to the seller only after the property is officially recorded in the buyer's name.

The company also provides title insurance, which is an insurance policy that will cover the buyer in the event there is an issue with the title that turns up later (rare but could happen). The seller of the property almost always covers the cost of this insurance during closing.

You should get to know a good escrow officer in your area. Also note that the seller and buyer do not have to close at the same title company; they each can use their own. Sometimes, the seller or buyer will specifically request a particular company to meet a special need. For example, if you are buying a property in a subdivision development, the contractor may want all the properties sold through the same title company because the title company is very familiar with the project.

Sometimes, the title company can only provide service in a particular market or state. Thus, if you buy elsewhere, you will need to use a different title company.

Years ago, I did a split closing (buyer and seller used separate title companies). During the close, the escrow agent I had used for years said, "Kirk, I think the other title company has made an error." After a thorough review and a few phone calls, we learned she was correct. She saved us over $20,000 that very day.

Most closings now are done online. If it is your first or second closing, I would suggest you go in person to have the experience and learn how the close works. The experience will help you with future real estate transactions.

Like all good sports teams, having the best players you can get on your team is key to your success. If you let someone else choose your players and assemble bad players, your results will probably turn out bad. There are plenty of players that are interested in taking your money for their services; however, you want to select the very best players that have your interest in mind, not just their own.

CHAPTER 12

Rags to Rental
Property—a Summary

A number of years ago, while I was the CEO of the property management company, I took both of our teenage sons to a real estate trade show with me in Los Angeles. During one stretch of the event, I took my youngest son with me to a breakout session on lending and left my older son (who was sixteen at that time) in the sales booth with one of our sales associates in the exhibit hall. Our company had sponsored a booth to promote selling property management franchises.

Around noon, I came back to the booth to see how my older son was holding up. He was so excited to tell me he had sold a franchise. I found that very difficult to believe because of the complexity of selling a franchise. You have to convince the buyer to give the franchisor tens of thousands of dollars, quit their job, and let the buyer know that they are probably going to work for a year or two with no income until they get the business established—a difficult sales task.

But my son told me the potential buyer wanted to meet his dad, the CEO, at two o'clock at the booth. I wasn't sure this was real, but I left the booth and returned at two o'clock. True to my son's word, there was a gentleman standing at the booth talking with my son and waiting for me to arrive. After I introduced myself, the first thing the man said was "This kid was so passionate about property management and what he was selling I just had to come and meet his dad and look into buying a franchise!"

Like my sixteen-year-old son, get *passionate* about being a real estate investor! You can do it. It is not that hard. Millions have done it and made millions of dollars. Yes, even regular people like you can do it. (My son still reminds me to this day that I owe him a sales commission for selling a franchise in LA.)

Perfectionism can kill. What I mean by that is, if you are only willing to purchase the perfect property, that day is not coming because a perfect property doesn't exist. The perfect property would be a twelve-thousand-square-foot mansion with an asking price of zero; again, that property doesn't exist. There will almost always be some issue, like maintenance or price or location and whatnot. You just need to build into the price or management of the property a way around the issue, if possible. Do not get tripped up over nickels and forego dollars.

Of all the information we have covered in this book, there are exceptions to almost everything discussed. Again, do not get tripped up on exceptions; look for ways around the exceptions to get a deal done, if possible.

Many potential investors want to purchase real estate when the prices are at rock bottom and then sell the property when it hits its peak price. But knowing exactly when those points occur is difficult, even with a crystal ball and tarot cards. And if you find a great deal like that and make $100,000 over a couple of years, you may not find another one for years. Why not find a pretty good deal, sell it for a nice profit a couple of years later, and make $50,000? But find and do five of these. You will make 5 × $50,000 = $250,000, versus the person that only found one amazing deal and made $100,000. In other words, you made 2.5 times more money than the person who is only willing to purchase the "amazing deals." We call this churning.

Never stop learning. There are many sources of information online and elsewhere. Become an expert in the various areas: lending, contracts, maintenance, etc. I've been involved in real estate for over forty years (we bought our first house when I was still in college), and I'm still learning new things about real estate every day. I read lots of articles, attend trade shows, subscribe to various services, and listen to people in the industry. I like knowing what the economic future is looking like, whether that is knowing a particular real estate market or knowing how a new tax law might affect real estate. You should do the same. A good friend of mine and a very successful real estate investor from the San Francisco area put it this way: "I'm a lifer in real estate," meaning, he is always looking at buying, selling, learning about, or helping others in real estate.

Need a place to start your real estate investing life? Take the assignments given in this book: (1) Get prequalified for a loan so you know how much you can borrow and thus how much you can offer on buying a property. This will cost you nothing. (2) Start scouring the Internet for properties in your area. It will only take a few minutes a day, and you will become an expert on property prices in your area very quickly. This, too, will cost you nothing. (3) Get a copy of a blank sales agreement from your favorite real estate agent and review it so that you are familiar with the various components. I'm sure your agent would be glad to assist you in reviewing the agreement, again costing you nothing. (4) Get a financial calculator on your phone. This will assist you in calculating mortgage payments.

The next steps are quite simple as well. First, you need to find the right property. Second, you want to make sure that your financing for the property is sound. Third, negotiate the deal quickly. Fourth, use your team of experts as needed. Fifth, act decisively. Don't think about it so long that either the deal goes away or you talk yourself out of it. The deal will either be good or not. Engage if the deal works; walk away if the numbers just don't work on the deal.

Someone once asked Bill Marriott, former CEO of Marriott International and owner of lots of real estate, when the best time to purchase real estate was. His answer is a classic: "Twenty years ago or today." In other words, get going now!

Remember the story of Bill, the tenant who was so excited to retire so he could start enjoying life? He died just a couple of weeks after retiring. Don't drive down Bill's road hoping someday, you can retire and then start to enjoy life. You can start enjoying life now. Have some fun. Don't take things too seriously. As you become a successful real estate investor, you can achieve a greater quality of life: more time to spend the way you choose, less stress and improved health, and more financial means to bless lives—yours, your family's, and many others'. Going from rags to rental property richness is within your grasp. Grab it!

ABOUT THE AUTHOR

 Born in Shelley, Idaho, Kirk grew up on a potato farm. This gave him many opportunities to learn how to both work hard and play hard. Later, after spending a couple of years living in Japan, he returned and attended school at Brigham Young University, where he earned his bachelor's degree in accounting. He then continued on at the University of Utah, earning a master's degree in business administration.

During those college years, he had earned a full scholarship with the Marriott Foundation. However, that was not enough money to keep everything going, so he took a job as a dishwasher and pizza delivery guy at a local restaurant. One day, his college roommate asked if he would be interested in starting a small business together. He was so glad to have an opportunity to quit dishwashing and pizza delivery that he said yes before he even knew what the business opportunity was. It turned out to be property management, which he knew nothing about.

In 1986, Kirk; his wife, Blenda; and his parents started a property management company, drawing on experience from his college days. But he had also started a software company that same year and spent most of his time with the software company. In 1996, the software company was sold, and full attention was given to property management.

Over the next couple of decades, the property management company grew to become the largest single-family residential property management company in North America, with over three hundred offices in the US and twenty-plus in Canada. These offices managed some $15 billion in real estate assets.

In 2012, Kirk was named Ernst & Young Regional Entrepreneur of the Year in real estate. In 2014, *Forbes* magazine named the property management company founded by Kirk as the tenth best franchise company in the US under $150,000 investment. *Entrepreneur* magazine named the company the best property management company in the US in 2015. And the company made it onto *Inc.* magazine's Inc. 500 list of the fastest-growing companies in the US four years in a row.

Now somewhat retired (can't quite get property management completely out of his system), Kirk spends much of his time investing in real estate and helping others change their financial lives by investing in real estate as well.

CPSIA information can be obtained
at www.ICGtesting.com
Printed in the USA
BVHW081735291121
622774BV00001B/59